KU-469-416

KNIVES IN HENS

David Harrower

Methuen Drama

QUEEN MARGARET COLLEGE LIBRARY

A Methuen Fast Track Playscript

First published in Great Britain in 1995
by Methuen Drama
an imprint of Reed International Books Ltd
Michelin House, 81 Fulham Road, London SW3 6RB
and Auckland, Melbourne, Singapore and Toronto

Reprinted 1996

Knives in Hens copyright © 1995 by David Harrower
The author has asserted his moral rights

ISBN 0 413 70510 2

A CIP catalogue record for this book is available from the
British Library

Typeset by Wilmaset Ltd, Birkenhead, Wirral
Printed in Great Britain by Intype London Ltd

Caution
All rights in this play are strictly reserved and application
for performance etc. should be made to the author's agent:
Casarotto Ramsay Ltd, National House, 60–66 Wardour Street,
London W1V 3HP. No performance may be given unless a
licence has been obtained.

This paperback is sold subject to the condition that it shall not,
by way of trade or otherwise, be lent, resold, hired out, or
otherwise circulated without the publisher's prior consent in any
form of binding or cover other than that in which it is published
and without a similar condition being imposed on the
subsequent purchaser.

for George Gunn

Knives in Hens was commissioned by and first performed at the Traverse Theatre, Edinburgh, on 2 June 1995 and transferred to the Bush Theatre, London, on 28 November 1995. The cast was as follows:

Young Woman	Pauline Knowles
Pony William	Lewis Howden
Gilbert Horn	Michael Nardone

Directed by Philip Howard
Designed by Mark Leese
Music composed and performed by Martyn Bennett

Characters

Young Woman, *a fieldhand*
Pony William, *a ploughman*
Gilbert Horn, *a miller*

Scene One

Rural place.

Cottage at the end of a village. Evening.

Young Woman   I'm not a field. How'm I a field? What's a field? Flat. Wet. Black with rain. I'm no field.

William   Never said that.

Young Woman   Says I'm a field sitting here.

William   Said you're like a field.

Young Woman   Said I'm a field sitting here.

William   Said you're like a field. Like a field.

Young Woman   'S the same.

William   Nothing close, woman.

Young Woman   If I'm like a field must be a field.

William (*laughs*)   Don't have to be a thing to be like it.

Young Woman   How?

William   Just don't.

Young Woman   'M I other things? Fire?

William   I got mud for feet. Can't feel them.

Young Woman   . . . Shoe? Bed? Door?

William   'S what it's for . . . Like.

Young Woman   Never heard it 'fore.

William   Like, woman. The moon's like cheese. 'S like cheese. But it's not.

Young Woman   You been up there? The moon's the moon. Why's it like cheese?

William   Always been said. (*Hears something.*) What's that? The horses?

Young Woman   So's cheese like the moon?

William Nnh. I'll go in and see them. They're not right.

Young Woman 'S cheese like the moon?

William I know more'n you.

Young Woman Know that.

William You're like any thing I want. I say you were like a field. You were like it, sitting there. Not now. 'S gone. You're not like this field sitting there now.

Young Woman Tell you what I'm like. I'm like nothing but me.

William You got a good shape.

Young Woman You got a good shape.

William Good shape now. Best in the village.

Young Woman 'S that field? (*He feels her.*) You tell me. 'S that field?

William You haven't seen the field.

Young Woman This's one field?

William Not many in the village know it.

Young Woman Where's it?

William Out-bye.

Young Woman I work on fields all over.

William Walk that way.

Young Woman Have before now.

William 'S the furthest over. The last field.

Young Woman I seen every field there is.

William 'S a good field. Good size. In all my years I've never seen it cheat or be stubborn or hold a grudge like others. Was made for a man, a horse and a plough. 'S flat and good 'til its end when it slopes but nothing that tires you. The soil's good and rich – so crops grow out the same. When it's rested the grass that grow's good too, and's the sweetest anywhere round here. Horses'll tell you that after grazing. See now, woman.

Young Woman   I'll walk to it one day. Walk back and tell you what I seen.

William   I need washing 'fore I go to the horses.

Young Woman (*as she leaves*)   Cheese the other women make's like the moon. My cheese's like cheese.

William   Before, I lay there and the horses'd be grazing slowly around me. Once I looked up and all that's my body'd gone inside out. All that's me on a circle of out-bye grass. Red. Wet. Rabbit hearts tied up with cow's saliva. I've never said a thing. Clouds came off me same's when I've pulled a new horse out in December. Nearly gone now, that. 'Fore it got dark I led them back, down the village to the stables, with this field still in my head. Why'd it come to me? Was only a boy. Could've lived in that field all my life if they let me. Mud's stinking.

Scene Two

Open ground.

Young Woman *enters carrying a basket.*

Young Woman   The wind blows. The sun shines. The crops grow. The sky – . . . The bird – flies. The clouds – . . . The tree . . . What? Stands. The tree stands. The sky – . . . The sky – . . . The rabbit runs. The clouds – . . . run? . . . grow? The leaves on the tree – . . . hang? The sky – . . . The sky – . . .

Scene Three

Fields.

William *in shirtsleeves, eating.* **Young Woman** *sits. Between them, the uncovered basket.*

William   You ill?

Young Woman   No.

William   Fever?

Young Woman   No.

William   What? Something wrong with you.

Young Woman   Nothing.

William   Seen you.

Young Woman   Walking to here. With food for you and the plough-horse.

William   Seen you standing there. What you doing?

Young Woman   I was looking. I was looking at . . .

William   What . . . ?

Young Woman   I saw a . . . a puddle, a puddle you can see the earth under. Clear water puddle after fresh rain. See the cracks in the earth there. See birdsfeet. See the sun shining. You got a name for that?

William   Puddle.

Young Woman   No. The right name.

William   Right name's puddle.

Young Woman   How?

William   You go straight to places, woman. You walk and don't stand.

Young Woman   Puddle's dark, mud water. See nothing in it. What was that I saw? Clear shining water. What?

William   Puddle. Still puddle. I've said 'fore. Dark puddle, clear puddle. 'S the same.

Young Woman   Things change each time I look at them.

William   Some do. Some don't. Keep with what you know. Best way. No standing looking. Village'll see. And talk. You know this village.

Young Woman   I don't know much. Don't know enough. When the wind makes the tree do this . . . (*Shakes herself.*) What's that? There a name for that? Why's it do it? See straight under the leaves then. Dunno'f it's right to look. What's that?

William   You'll get them. You'll get to know. You doubt God?

Young Woman   No. Never doubt God.

William   You're young still, 's why. I'm not. You'll get to know. Hear me? No more of it. What you done this morning?

Young Woman   After you left, I killed two hens and fed the rest. I gave one away for a bag of salt; the other I hung over the fire to dry. I pulled four potatoes from the earth and washed them. I drew fresh water from the well. I poured a candle with the last of the tallow. I dropped a knife on the cottage floor. I tanned a hide. I boiled stones in butter and kept the sauce. I weaved a blanket for our winter bed. I combed my hair for lice. I dropped to my knees and prayed. I stared at my hands. I brought food to you and the horse.

He eats, raises brow at the dropped knife, looks to the horse.

William   We've worked each other hard since sun-up. You not eating?

Young Woman   I'll watch you. 'S better. Eat's a horse.

He imitates a masticating horse — uncannily. She laughs.

William   I could eat more'f this food. 'S one thing you'll find every one has in common. Every one likes to eat. Never met man or woman who hasn't. Even them in other parts, they like it.

Young Woman   'S that what's in your head when you plough? 'S that what you see? Other places. Other people. Eating.

William   All ploughmen get tired of looking down at the earth. Black. Hurts the back and neck. Looked left or right they'd fall. I look up at the sky. But it hurts my neck and eyes.

Young Woman   We're not to look up there long. Our faces'd be on top of our heads, flat, if we were.

William   Know that.

Young Woman   God watches every thing. He sees every thing. He has the names for every thing.

William   'S right. Our faces are here, north side, to look straight ahead.

Young Woman   There's all we need to look at between our earth and his sky. I'm glad's us.

William   Glad's us what?

Young Woman   Glad's us got married. If I hadn't married you I'd have married someone else but it wouldn't be the same. Said that soon's I seen you.

William   Pour me some milk.

Young Woman   Like kissing your cock.

William   Here. Eat.

Scene Four

Outside cottage.

Very early morning. **Young Woman** *calling, walks to the stable.*

Young Woman   William? William?

William   Ssh. Ssh. There. All right now. Quiet.

Young Woman   William, William, will-he-be-here? William, William, will-he-be-there? (*Enters.*) William!

William   SHUT YOUR MOUTH WOMAN OR BY GOD HIMSELF I'LL DO IT FOR YOU!!!! Woman? . . . 'S what I said day we married. You don't come in the stable without asking me. Puts the fear in the horses. They dunno what't is. Scares them.

Young Woman   Sorry, William . . . How long till I can?

William   Don't speak for horses. Could be another summer. They got to trust your smell. And your voice. Each of them.

Young Woman   . . . Where're you?

William   Stall on the end.

Young Woman   The bed was empty. And cold.

William   I was out most'f the night.

Young Woman (*moving further in*)   What's . . . ?

William   Stay back! This mare, she's in trouble. She's shaking.

Young Woman   She dying?

William   No. She got a young one inside her.

Young Woman   That it?

William   'S her first time, woman.

Young Woman   You be's quick when I'm carrying our first.

William   Go in, woman. 'S cold.

Young Woman   Know which one it was?

William   Him there. Told him to stay away. (*To horse.*) You know that's what I said. Stay away. Last time I trust that one. Now go in.

Young Woman   You coming in?

William   Told you. She needs me here.

Young Woman   Not having it now's she?

William   No. But I'm not leaving her. She dunno where she is. She's only a girl. (*Silence.*) Woman? You there?

Young Woman   Horses you want to be with, not me. Live in this stable.

William   This's me, woman. You know that.

Young Woman   There's boys in the village'd help you.

William   Don't want 'em. These horses are special. Boys aren't. 'S you I want with me. And you'll do it. Now go'n eat. 'S you doing my work today.

Young Woman   What's wanting done?

William   Must know that. Grain. 'S needing ground.

Young Woman   I've to go to the mill?

William   I'm staying with her.

Young Woman   Want me going out there?

William   'S what I said.

Young Woman   . . . Today?

William   You want it all to rot and us starve? Hh? The cart's loaded. 'N take bastard there. (*Horse.*) Away from me.

Young Woman   They say's him killed his wife and the child she was giving birth to. 'N there's disappeared men and women who're cats and goats and monkeys now. Go from market to market, sleeping together and singing for food.

William   He knows you've me. Knows what I'd do.

Young Woman   Since I was a girl they've talked of the miller.

William   All you need's hate for him. 'S what he expects. Every bone of your body. Hate. 'S a village custom.

Young Woman   I do hate him!

William   Again.

Young Woman   I HATE him!

William   Stronger!

Young Woman   I HATE HIM!! Show him you're afraid, 's how it starts. I hate every miller there is. Throw them in a pond and watch their bodies swell and stink.

William   You got it now. Eleventh of a peck, he gets. He can't steal more. You tell him – pull them sleeves up, miller.

Young Woman   Pull them sleeves up, miller!

William   . . . when he weighs the flour. Eleventh of a peck. Bastard. 'N you watch him. You watch our grain.

Scene Five

Mill. Soft sound of a river.

Young Woman *unloads the first grain-sack with much effort.* **Gilbert Horn** *appears, watches her. She becomes aware but carries on.*

Gilbert You wanting help with your sacks?

Young Woman (*low*) You stay away from me, boy.

Gilbert I said d'you want . . .

Young Woman No. Don't need help.

Gilbert Makes it . . .

Young Woman I do it alone!

Gilbert First time for you here. Fine horse. Bring them up to the door. You got a name for yourself? I'm Gilbert Horn. Your husband lying ill and useless in bed?

Young Woman He's in the fields, pushing a plough, fit and strong.

Gilbert His wife's a fair strength herself. Strength's right in a woman.

Young Woman Leave it! Don't want you near my sacks.

Does her best to glare at him. He goes into the mill. She fetches the last sack, peers into the mill.

Gilbert The mill-stone. Beautiful. No?

Young Woman Where's the grain go?

Gilbert There. Empty your first in. I'll open the river for the wheel. Then go and sit in my house.

Young Woman I'm standing here.

Gilbert The stone's old. Takes time.

Young Woman Right here, I said.

Gilbert When it turns you want no ears.

Young Woman Standing here till I see my flour.

He goes. Wheel starts to turn. The noise grows, becomes deafening. She endures it, shaking, hands to her ears. Finally runs out.

Scene Six

Gilbert's *cottage.*

He sits at a table. **Young Woman** *comes to the threshold.*

Young Woman   Freezing in there.

Gilbert   You want some ale. A dram? (*Shakes her head.*) Coming in or staying there?

Young Woman   Stand right where I am.

Gilbert   You won't care if I take a drop?

Young Woman   Don't care any thing you do. 'S your house.

He drinks, then yawn-shouts.

Gilbert   Aaauuhhhh. Oh . . . work . . . work . . . work . . .

Young Woman   Must break your back that stone doing the work.

Gilbert   Ih?

Silence. He drinks more.

Takes special men to be millers. Men who work hard. Alone. In ways villages know nothing of.

Long silence. Finally points to the door.

See that? There. There. 'S a name. You know it? Door-stump. That's my door-stump . . . 'S that not what your village believes?

Young Woman   What?

Gilbert   When a thing's got a name 's got a use?

Young Woman   Dunno what you're . . . Not getting me to shut this door, miller-man.

Gilbert   Stop that cold air freezing up 'my house'.

Young Woman   I want to see my grain.

Gilbert   'S staying there.

Young Woman   I came with five sacks . . .

Gilbert   Well counted.

Young Woman   I'm leaving with five sacks.

Gilbert   How'd I get it sat here?

He gets up for more drink. Begins to whistle softly. She's getting more frantic, watching her grain, watching him.

Young Woman   You stop! Stop!

Gilbert   Ih?

Young Woman   Get my husband out to you, boy! Said stop! . . . Why you laughing? STOP!!

Gilbert   They got another living in the ground. Dirt in your eyes, field-hand. Mouth flapping in the wind. Ears open. Shovels filled them with the names of Gilbert Horn. What you got rotting in there?

Young Woman   I got nothing there.

Gilbert   No? Not the power of magic I have? The death charms? Not which plants're to be picked special. Not which bones and eyes of animals and birds need kept and powdered? Nothing of my wife and child? Not that I killed them both? Not that I've no want of family? None've that in there?

Young Woman   Evil-breath!

Begins to inch out backwards.

Gilbert   Where you going, dung-brain?

Young Woman   Away from your evil, bastard.

Gilbert   That village's death. Nothing.

Young Woman   Not taking my eyes off you, boy. Not turning my back. You'll die you touch me.

He turns away, sits down again. She's almost out.

Gilbert   . . . 'S you married that Pony William, wasn't it?

She freezes.

'S who shares your bed. The village ploughman. Pony
William . . .

Young Woman   No. No.

Gilbert   No?

Young Woman   You leave him.

Gilbert   That not his name? Pony William.

Young Woman   'S name's William.

Gilbert   I hear Pony William.

Young Woman   You don't say that.

Gilbert   'S what most in the village call him.

Young Woman   Liar.

Gilbert   I hear them. Pony William –

Young Woman   Liar!

Gilbert   'N Pony's bride.

Young Woman   I'd spit on them say that.

Gilbert   Heard's 'cos of his love for the younger horses.

Young Woman   No . . .

Gilbert   No? . . . Just the one horse? Special horse?

Young Woman   . . . That's envy.

Gilbert   Envy? Not heard that spoke in a long time. 'S the
village tell you what it is?

Young Woman   'Course.

Gilbert   How's that envy?

Young Woman   Envy of us back there. In the village.

Gilbert   Envy of you and Pony and them others all living in a
death place? All them rotted lives? How've I envy?

Young Woman   I know. 'S a look. The eyes. Like evil.

Gilbert   Do it.

Young Woman   What?

Gilbert   Envy.

Young Woman   Can't.

Gilbert   Why?

Young Woman   Haven't got it. Stupid.

Gilbert   'S what they say.

Young Woman   Who?

Gilbert   'S that what you seen?

Young Woman   What?

Gilbert   Horses come first with him.

Young Woman   No. Loves me first.

Gilbert   First.

Young Woman   'N always.

Gilbert   Then you won't like it?

Young Woman   I like love. Better'n evil.

Gilbert   You don't like them calling him Pony William?

Young Woman   You leave that name I said.

Gilbert   You don't like Pony William.

Young Woman   NO. No.

Gilbert   Then there you are.

Young Woman   Where?

Gilbert   What power've you over other's tongues?

She leaves.

Scene Seven

Cottage.

William *comes on to find* **Young Woman** *there.*

William   Where's the flour? Horse's there. 'N the cart. Where's the flour?

Young Woman   The mill.

William   You left our sacks there, woman?

Young Woman   That miller's stone's old and weak. Stood freezing as he sat.

William   All my grain left with that miller . . .

Young Woman   You take the cart tomorrow. Be ground then. Ready.

William   You go back.

Young Woman   Still our flour tomorrow.

William   Go back. Take the horse and cart and get our grain.

She doesn't move.

Had my eye on you for years. Watched you grow. Picked you to be my wife. Be my good, strong wife. Who'd work same's me. Who'd sweat same's me. Who'd not run when she's afraid.

Young Woman   I didn't run!

William   Can see it. You got the fear of him in you. Where's the hate? Hh? Told you hate.

Young Woman   . . . I had it. Going there. But's him. Close by. Looking.

William   Watch the stone, hate the man.

Young Woman   'N he talks and talks.

William   Always does that. What'd he say? What's he talking now?

Young Woman   . . . Nothing.

William   'S right. All he's got's that mouth. Woman, listen to the stone, not the miller. Talk. 'S all he's got. All day and all night to no one. 'S nothing. Now go back. Go. Be my wife.

Scene Eight

Countryside.

Young Woman   The sun warms the wind that blows. The wind pushes the clouds under the sky. Black cloud holds the rain. White cloud . . . The bird flies under the white cloud – into the tree. Tree's for wood. The bird's for . . . One bird. One's lucky, two's unlucky, three's health, four's wealth, five's sickness, and six is death. Dead bird, bake a pie. The wind pushes the white cloud under the sun. White cloud's for . . . The rabbit runs on the field. Rabbit's food. The bird – the tree . . . loses the bird. Bird's gone. The wind pushes the white cloud off the sun. White cloud's for . . . White cloud's for . . .

Scene Nine

Gilbert's *house.*

Gilbert *sits at his table, writing on paper with an ink pen.* **Young Woman** *appears, remains in the doorway. She watches him and also the pen. Finally he looks up, across at her.*

Gilbert   Still five. You counted? Still five there, ih? (*Pause.*) Last sack's on.

Young Woman   I seen that.

Gilbert   Where'd you go?

Young Woman   Had other work to do. Couldn't stand wasting time. Hearing talk about nothing.

Gilbert   Won't be long to stand now.

Pause.

Young Woman   'S a new stone you need, miller. I'm wanting to get home 'fore the sky goes black.

Gilbert   Stonemason's nearly finished the new one. When he's done your village men'll roll it out here, to me.

He writes again.

Young Woman   ... What you got there?

Gilbert   What?

Young Woman   ... that.

Gilbert   This? You don't know what this is? 'S a pen. Ink pen.

Young Woman   What you wanting with that?

Gilbert   Sold to me at market by a travelling musician.

Young Woman   Food-money spent on a useless stick.

Gilbert   'S worth the price.

Young Woman   Flour you steal from us 's what bought it.

Gilbert   See how the firelight shines on it.

Young Woman   What's it – feed you?

Gilbert   No.

Young Woman   Warm you?

Gilbert   'S a good weight in the hand.

Young Woman   Waste.

Gilbert   Write with it too.

Young Woman   What?

Gilbert   I ... write ...

Young Woman   What d'you write?

Gilbert   What I've done.

Young Woman   Grind corn. Stop grinding corn. Grind corn. Stop grinding corn.

Gilbert   More'n that.

Young Woman   Must be the laird's new game. Only he'd write down the nothing he does. You wanting to be the laird now, miller?

Gilbert   I've more life than corn. I write what's in here, in my head. End of the day, every day. Here . . . to here.

Holds up a sheaf of papers.

Look how much of me there is. Can tell what's in my head yesterday, or . . . last winter, and most days since.

Young Woman   Then's an evil trick!

Gilbert   Evil?

Young Woman   Ready for the fire.

Gilbert   Evil – this? How?

Young Woman   'S God puts things in your head and's him who takes them away. 'S sin to keep them.

Gilbert   Field-hand, could not be God gave us this . . .

Young Woman   Not us.

Gilbert   . . . so's we can know more'f the world?

Young Woman   'S an evil stick you made.

Gilbert   I can tell who's come to my mill, who's stood outside, who's come in to drink, who's said not a word, who's cursed me over and over, who's stood in my doorway, who's been so afraid of Gilbert Horn they turned and ran back to the village with their husband's . . . (*Writes.*) . . . horse and cart.

Pause. She realises.

Young Woman   You take that off there!

Gilbert   Ink's dry now.

Young Woman   . . . Then burn it. Do it, bastard! Give it to the fire.

Gilbert   I thank him I wasn't born in that village. 'S a black pit. Pulled from the womb older'n when you die. Elders stand at the bed-end and use knives to drain away the blood. Dark night's what's left round your bones. Pull out eyes and leave cold pebbles in the hollows.

Young Woman   You reek of evil filth words, boy!

Gilbert   Evil – what else's a villager say faced with a man got eyes and tongue who're trusted friends? Man who looks slow and close at the world for all the names it's got. 'Sky's going black?' Not over me. I live under different sky.

Young Woman   'S earth we'll put you under – fill you over. Stop up that mouth.

Gilbert   I'll be you then. Under earth. Seeing nothing out pebble eyes. Seeing nothing.

Young Woman   I see.

Gilbert   Knowing nothing.

Young Woman   I see. Know what I see.

Gilbert   Track. Mud. Horse. Here. There. Sky ...

Young Woman   See more'n that. I got names for most things in God's world.

Gilbert   Tell me what.

Young Woman   I'll tell you nothing. Not giving you what's in my head.

Gilbert   Stink of shit, 's why.

Young Woman   I got things ... I got things. Not speaking them.

Gilbert *leans over, places the pen on side of table nearest to her.*

Gilbert   Then write them.

Young Woman   Not touching that ...

Gilbert   Write what you seen coming to my mill. Show me the village's more'n peasants with rotting shit in their heads.

Young Woman   Stone you for that.

Gilbert   'Course ...

Young Woman You wanting stoned? I'll tell them.

Gilbert Can't write.

Young Woman I can write, boy!

Gilbert Prove it. (*Shakes her head.*) How's this evil? You write.

Young Woman 'S chalk we had.

Gilbert Pen's better chalk.

Young Woman Still not getting any thing from my head.

Gilbert What'll I do? Only ink on paper.

Young Woman Dunno. Some thing.

Gilbert After you write I'll put it in the fire.

Young Woman 'S tricks.

Gilbert Then you take it. Carry it home. Show Pony what you can do.

Young Woman *hesitates.*

Young Woman No . . . Why d'you want what's in here? 'S mine.

Gilbert How'll anyone ever know? (*Silence.*) You can write, ih?

Young Woman Said I could.

Gilbert Then give me something outside you. That all the village knows.

Young Woman What you wanting, miller?

Gilbert . . . Your name.

Silence. Finally she comes to the table. A sheet of pearl-white paper skates towards her.

Young Woman No tricks.

Gilbert None.

She has difficulty mastering the pen. Resolute.

Young Woman Show you I'm no dung-brain.

He tries to draw the paper to him. She slams a fist on it, holds it up so he can read it.

Gilbert   Tell you what, horse-wife. You're beautifully named.

They look at each other. He gets up. She moves back to the door with the paper. He walks towards her.

Your flour's ready. I got to take what's mine.

Scene Ten

Cottage.

William   Here's wife. She've any more trouble with Killer-miller? (*Shakes her head.*) She stable the horse right? (*Nod.*) She come back with our five sacks? (*Nod.*) She keep a close eye on the flour? (*Nod.*) She wanting a bowl of meal? (*Shake.*) She'll find them husks get everywhere. She'll feel they're growing under her skin. She'll find water to wash with. She'll be thankful for her husband's hand.

She goes to the water. Wearily looks down at herself, gives a small scream when she sees the black marks that are on the thumb and forefinger of one hand.

Young Woman   Auh . . . !

William   . . . What's it, woman?

Young Woman *freezes.*

Young Woman   Spark. From the fire. William, we can go straight to bed.

William   No washing?

Young Woman   Could you not take sweat and roughness on you for a night?

William's *eyes widen, grins.*

William   No better words spoke since we wed.

Young Woman   Lie down. I'll be quick.

He crosses to the bed. She dips her fingers in the water, starts rubbing.
William *whistles as he undresses and gets on the bed. A laughing vision of* **Gilbert** *now appears, wearing a dazzling-white miller's apron. At his feet a sack of flour.*

William   You coming, woman?

Young Woman   I'm there, William, I'm . . .

She closes her eyes trying to get rid of him. Concurrent sound of rubbing hands, **William**'s *whistling,* **Gilbert**'s *just-audible laughter.*

How's the mare, William?

William   She's better . . .

Young Woman   O Sweet God in Heaven . . .

William   You saying, woman?

Gilbert *vanishes.*

Young Woman   Prayer before bed, William.

William   Best you do. Once you're down here, God can't help.

Snorts at his prurient wit. Fingers clean, she goes to the bed.

Scene Eleven

Same.

Darkness before dawn. **Gilbert**'s *vision reappeared. Takes flour from sack, claps hands. Great flour-clouds in the air.* **Young Woman** *in a loose shift moves in her sleep, sneezes and wakes.*

Young Woman   . . . ! Out this house! You! Out! William, run him out. William.

Turns to wake **William***: bed's empty.*

What you done with him . . . ? I'll fetch him in. He'll rid you! He'll finish you!

Runs out to the stables. Approaches door, pauses, listens, raises her hand to knock. Before she can, **William**'s *voice is heard.*

William   'S it, sweet. You're a lovely one. A good one.

Young Woman *softens, shoulders drop. Smiles with joy, relief.*

Young Woman   Sweet God in Heaven, the foal's come. Oh. Thank you.

Again **William***'s soft, warm voice. She listens, enjoying it.*

William   Take your time . . . good and slow . . . you're a lovely one, a lovely one. O, my sweet.

From within comes female laughter. **Young Woman** *stares at the stable doors. The laugh again. She runs into the house, looking for* **Gilbert***. Goes to her clothes, then out the house and off.*

Scene Twelve

Before dawn. Countryside.

Young Woman   When the sun comes back the warm wind will blow on my face. When I look up I will see the sun shine bright on the sky. The clouds will . . . be white. The crops . . . the strong crops will grow on the good field. The bird will sing on the tall tree. The tall tree will . . . stand and the warm wind will shake the leaves. The rabbit will run on the good field where the strong crops grow. New day will start and end the night. Night will be gone.

Scene Thirteen

Gilbert*'s house.*

Young Woman   Bastard! You open up! Take it off!

Gilbert   . . . Ploughman, you there? I never touched her. Never would. Know she's yours.

Young Woman   You know where he's, miller. You charmed him. Only me here. Only me here, filth. Open your door. Stand here till you do, boy. (*Door opens.*) You take it off us, miller! You take it off!

Gilbert What you wanting?

Young Woman Take your charm off me and my ploughman. What we done?

Gilbert You're talking madness.

Young Woman You got envy of us! See it now. In the eyes.

Gilbert Go home.

Young Woman I'll get other men out here. You do it with this, ih? Tricker. Water washed it off. Can't be a strong charm. Got in my head. Climbed in. Laughing. Throwing flour over us. 'S your magic. Charming him out to the stables. Making your laugh a woman's. That it gone now?

She's torn the paper as she spoke.

Gilbert A woman's laugh?

Young Woman That it gone? Tell me, miller.

Gilbert D'you look in the stables, horse-wife?

Young Woman Wasn't looking at any more'f your tricks.

Gilbert A woman's laugh. Ha ha.

Young Woman Take it off, miller . . . Please. Beg you. You want to lie with me? That it. Leave us then. Here. Pleasure for you under here, miller.

Gilbert Get up . . . All I need's to kiss you.

She goes to kiss him. He gets lost in it, in her.

Young Woman Gone now, oh . . . 'S it off, miller, ih? (*He shrugs.*) What's that? 'S gone now.

Gilbert Dunno. Just wanted to kiss you. Only charm I know.

As he grins, he's violently punched by **Young Woman**, *falls.*

Young Woman O God make this man die in cold pain! Evil!

Gilbert FUCK OFF YOU! I got no magic! FUCK OFF AWAY FROM ME! Fuck off back to your silent village! Fuck off back to your greedy man! 'N run! RUN!! You'll catch the Robertson girl still licking on his tired cock.

Young Woman *has backed away. He slams the door. She stands still, alone outside his house.*

Scene Fourteen

Gilbert's *house.*

Much later. **Young Woman** *still outside.* **Gilbert** *comes to put a blanket around her. She turns and walks into the house, sits at the table, picks up the pen, begins writing on the sheets of paper there.*

Scene Fifteen

Inside **Gilbert**'s *house.*

Young Woman *wakes from sleep at the table, aware of his blanket around her.*

Gilbert   'S evening. Better'n any bed, that soft paper. Lay down on it myself.

Young Woman   Why'm I here? What you done to me?

Gilbert   Nothing. You held the pen yourself.

Young Woman *looks at the pen, sees the paper, reads.*

Young Woman   'This is me. I live now. Others have, more will. I was born here because God wanted it. He had me sit in my mother till I could look at all that is His world. Every thing I see and know is put in my head by God. Every thing He created is there every day, sunrise to sundown, earth to sky. It cannot be touched or held the way I touch a table or hold the reins of a horse. It cannot be sold or cooked. His world is there, in front of my eyes. All I must do is push names into what is there the same as when I push my knife into the stomach of a hen. This is how I know God is there. I look at a tree and say tree then walk on. The tree is God. It is always God. But there is more. I know there is more of the tree that is God which I have no names for. Every name I have will take me closer to Him. This is how I will know God better. A puddle I can see under. A tree when it is blown by the wind. A carrot that is sweeter than the others. The cold earth under a rock. The warm breath of a tired horse. A man's face in the evening after work. The sound a woman makes when no one hears her. Only when I am deserving will I learn the names. This is what the village has always said. I know now I must find out the names for myself. If I stand and look close at every thing God will reward me. This is how I will know God better. The village has lied. William has lied. It is not because I am young and they are old. God has given them nothing. I know this now. I see William ploughing a field. I do not have a name for the thing which is in my head. It is not envy. It is more than envy. It does not scare me. I must look close enough to discover what it is. Every thing in my head is put there by God. Every name I have will take me closer to Him.' This was me.

Gilbert   All afternoon you wrote.

She picks up the pen and begins writing again.

Young Woman   'S not envy. No. What is it? What is it? What's this thing? (*Finishes writing.*) William. Tell me 's not you done this.

Gilbert   No. I stood here and watched you.

Young Woman   I've no torment or misery. Then it is God. It is God.

She sheds the blanket, walks to the door, looks at him, goes out. He stares at what she's written.

Scene Sixteen

Cottage. Night.

William *in bed, dozing.* **Young Woman** *standing above him.*

William   ...'S that? You? ... Woman ...?

Young Woman   Yes, William.

William   Haw... Where you been?

Young Woman   The last field.

William   Hh?

Young Woman   The furthest over. Said I'd walk out to it one day. Come back and tell you what I seen.

William   You been gone the full day, woman . . .

Young Woman   I was praying.

William   For a full day?

Young Woman   For us, William. Praying for us and what we have. Was so beautiful I had to pray, William. Longer God's given the greater his reward. Asked for a full harvest, William.

William   'S good.

Young Woman   'N the horses to stand strong.

William   'S the right prayer.

Young Woman   'N the mare. Prayed for her.

William   Her foal'll be here by the week's end.

Young Woman   Don't want her hurting more. Or moaning. Like she does.

William   You tell me'f you go out there again.

Young Woman   I will.

William   You live here, you stay here. No going off and saying nothing.

He goes to her, arms around her.

'S good to feel you, woman. Whole village I searched for you. 'You seen my woman?' 'You seen my woman?'

Young Woman   What'd they say?

William   None had.

Young Woman   How far'd you come out the village, William?

William   Couldn't go far. I had a field to plough. And the new mill-stone pulled upright ready for rolling tomorrow.

Young Woman   Tomorrow?

William   'S why I needed you back. 'S our first 'rolling-of-the-stone' as man and wife. Us men need you women to shout us on. Now come to bed, woman.

Young Woman   I had to go, William. Had to see this field. You were right. It is like me. 'S a beautiful field.

William   'S what I said. Now come down, woman, come down.

Young Woman   You need washing 'fore sleep, William?

William   No.

Young Woman   You done it?

William   No wife here to help. Not take roughness and sweat on you for a night?

Later in the night.

Gilbert *has appeared again.* **Young Woman** *moves pleasurably on the bed, eyes open. She crosses to take flour from the sack, rubs it on herself.* **William** *screams in his sleep.*

William   Uuaaaghhh!! Uh . . . oh.

Gilbert *disappears. She returns to the bed.*

Young Woman   William.

William   Oh . . . You not hear it, woman? 'S falling off you. Oh.

Young Woman   What?

William   Skin . . . your skin . . . I'd my hands on you, touching and it came off . . . like cattle hide. Dry. Oh. Tore off warm. Left you with holes all over, and . . . your eyes never opened. You not hear it, woman? Tearing. Oh. You not hear it? Oh. Needing water.

He stumbles away. She lies down.

Scene Seventeen

Village. Outside the stonemason's.

Noise of villagers. **William** *and* **Young Woman**.

William   Look at the rock! Look at its size. Stonemason! You've made your village proud. 'S the finest stone ever been carved. Stand back. Best time of year, this. All the village together. God knows. Given us the day for it. Shining sun and the west wind. 'S what we asked for. Hold yourself, miller, sitting alone in your mill. When the stone rolls, the earth thunders! Be sure and keep up, woman. Shout your stone-man on.

Scene Eighteen

Outside mill.

Young Woman *and* **William** *sit after the new mill-stone's been placed.* **Gilbert** *comes on carrying a whisky keg.*

William   What you want, miller? We rest now.

Gilbert   To thank the village for its labour and its sweat.

William   We roll the stone for us, miller. Our rent can only be paid with flour.

Young Woman   And our bread only baked with it.

Gilbert   Will you've a miller's dram of gratitude?

William   Have others drunk it?

Gilbert   Some have, some haven't.

William   I'll try your potion, miller.

Young Woman   William, make him drink it first.

Gilbert *drinks, proffers it to* **William**.

Gilbert   She's a beautiful stone . . . more than stone – monument. A second church. Carved from love and life in equal parts.

Young Woman   'N who takes it? The most undeserving.

William *laughs*.

Gilbert   Will your woman take a drop?

William   Will you, woman?

Young Woman   I will. 'S water, not whisky! Weak and cold.

William   Woman's right.

Young Woman   You wash in it, miller? That how you brew it?

Gilbert   Does me. Out here.

Young Woman   No one to help drink it, 's why.

William   I'll have more. Rid you of it.

Young Woman   You want good whisky, miller, come to the village. Buy from us.

William   Off now, miller. Leave us.

Young Woman *slumps to the ground*.

Woman . . . ? Woman! What you done, miller?!

Gilbert   . . . I done nothing.

William   This's you, I'll kill you.

Gilbert   Swear, ploughman. Sit her up . . .

William   Away from her! Woman . . . (*Feels her face*.) Stupid woman. Stupid. Standing on a field for a day. Too many prayers and no food. We've work to finish. Not wanting to see the old stone broken up?

Gilbert   Ploughman. I want it kept.

William   No. 'S old. Finished. This's work the men want.

Gilbert   'M asking you, ploughman. I want it kept. Was the last stone turned by me and my wife. (*Pause*.) Served me well. Served the village well.

William   Where you want it, miller? Rolled to your bed?

Gilbert   Behind the house's a shed. Stand it along the far wall.

William   Nnh.

Gilbert   'S a long walk home. I've a fire built inside. Your woman'd be better by its warmth.

William   'F you can, take her in. 'S work you know, miller. Carrying women.

Gilbert   My thanks again, ploughman.

William   Been told. Don't want your thanks. You be standing when I'm back, woman.

William *goes.* **Gilbert** *shouts to him.*

Gilbert   Ploughman! Tell your men to cover the face. Shed's my privy.

Turns to see **Young Woman** *sitting up. They both walk off.*

Scene Nineteen

Gilbert*'s house.*

Young Woman *lying on the bed.* **Gilbert** *stands over her.* **William** *comes in.*

William   She up? Woman? On your feet. Village's gone. Woman. You got nothing for her, miller? Give you money.

Gilbert   I've nothing.

William   'S night, woman. I need sleep. No horse have you, miller?

Gilbert   No need of one. Sleep here with her.

William   Can't sleep on any bed but my own.

Gilbert   Carry her yourself.

William   After two mill-stones and your whisky? (*Looks around.*) 'S where you sit your nights?

Gilbert   Front've a fire like you.

William   'N do what?

Gilbert   Eat. Sit. Read.

William   Why d'you have all them books?

Gilbert   So's when I finish one I can read another.

William   Smart. That why you got them standing up like that, touching? Don't look right. Nothing else here. Must feel the need of more, eh?

Gilbert   More of what?

William *indicates the* **Young Woman**.

Gilbert   . . . I'm a man like you.

William   You're a miller, miller. Not like me. Nothing like me.

Gilbert   'S only a special woman wants to know a miller. Most believe we've dead worms in our trousers.

William   More'n that, miller. More'n what's in the trousers. More hate'n that. Where you been?

Gilbert   Doesn't trouble me now, ploughman.

William   You must pray to be one of us, miller. The country over you're hated. Even the children run from you. Ever ask why that is? You get part of our grain for milling it. That's law. But we hate you more'n that law. We're stupid and cruel. Blind. Hate you more'n any thing I can name. Why's that, miller? Why's it like that? Your wife was a miller's daughter, wasn't she? Had to be. 'D she love you? . . . 'D you love her? How long since you seen a woman there, miller? Lying on her back. What you got in your head, looking at her? Look at her. Look. A new country. D'you remember the colours of it, how fallow it looks, how it takes your breath? Fresh earth. Mist. Grass around rock. D'you remember the smell? D'you remember the strength? How you believe you're destroying her with your shape, making a new land, God that you are. D'you remember how she turns? How she loses you? Legs. Neck. Stomach. Arms. Breast. Wrong names, they are, miller. Who named them? Never the same's

QUEEN MARGARET COLLEGE LIBRARY

men's. Never. Women've no legs. No arms. They've more. I got names for them. My own names. She knows. No one else.

Gilbert   Loved my wife.

William (*laughs*)   Village'd run me out for that talk.

Gilbert   Why?

William   You stand in church, same's me.

Gilbert   Never listen.

William   'The glory of God is God, not His creation.' 'S what they say now. I need to piss. You believe that, miller? Glory of God's God, not His creation.

Gilbert   Dunno.

William   'S that not God there? You look. 'S that not? You gone without too long. You look at it. You remember.

Gilbert   She's your wife.

William   I'm a ploughman, miller. Earth gets weak you keep turning it. You got to rest it. Always other fields to start on. – More God.

Gilbert   You know where's the shed. Walk to the sound of the river.

William   Fool you believe I'm going in this blackness.

He takes a candle and goes out. **Young Woman** *sits up, walks to the door and goes out.* **Gilbert** *follows.*

Scene Twenty

Shed.

William *using the privy. The old mill-stone in candlelight.* **Young Woman** *and* **Gilbert** *emerge from behind it, push the stone over.*

Scene Twenty-One

Gilbert's *house.*

Gilbert *and* **Young Woman** *sit opposite each other, watching the other slowly undress. From the shed come* **William**'s *faint death screams. The screams fade. They stand and walk to the bed.*

Scene Twenty-Two

Gilbert's *house.*

After. **Young Woman** *and* **Gilbert** *lying together.*

Young Woman   Filth ... Evil-breath ... Love. 'S near dawn. (*Pause.*) The morning I ran here, you said, you shouted at me ... ... Fuck ... Off.

Gilbert   Fuck off.

Young Woman   No one's ever said that to me. Never heard that before.

Gilbert   First time I've ever said it.

Young Woman   'S it mean?

Gilbert   Dunno. Was shouted at market. A Bible-seller back from Germany. A boy was pissing near his stall. (*Pause.*) What's in your head now?

Young Woman   Know that. You.

Gilbert   That all?

Young Woman   What? Pony William? Village ploughman? No. What've you got, in here?

Gilbert   Some thing ...

Young Woman   God saw. We're deserving now. He'll give us more 'f what He is. You feel it? New world front 'f us.

Gilbert   Before; standing there ... he said, your ploughman said -- 'What you got in your head, miller, looking at her?' You hear him? I saw my wife. Woman that was my wife. Then you were there. In here. My head. No clothes. Pushing. Sweating. Groaning like the wind. Eyes open, arms open, I was in your mouth, at your cunt, in your hair. 'S it God put you there? My body was like nothing I've known in my life. 'S it God did that?

Young Woman   'Course.

Gilbert   No . . . Not God. Was what your ploughman said. Was his words.

Young Woman   No.

Gilbert   His words made me do that. Was me.

Young Woman   All his talk's lies. Ploughman couldn't see.

Gilbert   I did that. In my own head.

Young Woman   Never knew nothing. I'm not like any thing. Look. You seen that. You seen that now.

Gilbert   Was me. You not understand, woman? Was me.

Young Woman   'S near dawn. I've to walk back.

Gilbert   After this?

Young Woman   Tell the village.

Gilbert   What?

Young Woman   William's gone.

Gilbert   'N have them come for me – your village.

Young Woman   The hated miller. No. Get a shovel. Body needs buried.

Gilbert   Saw him here last.

Young Woman   I'll tell them. Bed's empty and cold. Fields empty. Stables empty.

Gilbert   They'll still come.

Young Woman   No. Look. 'He's left me. He's gone for a better wife. He walked away in the night. I sit alone by the fire. Look at my tear puddles. I'm the broken-hearted wife.'

Gilbert   How long?

Young Woman   Until they believe.

Gilbert   You'll come back?

Young Woman   Live in the mill?

Gilbert   Live in the village? (*She goes.*) 'S not You. 'S me.

Scene Twenty-Three

Stables.

Young Woman *delivers the mare's pony.*

Young Woman   Sshh . . . Don't get scared. Feel my hands. Warm hands. Wife of William. Friend. Strong. Quiet. There. Breathe now. Sshh . . . Here it comes. Push, love, push. Head and neck. Eyes. Push a last time. Sssh . . . There. There. Look, mother . . . Life. A new horse in the world.

Scene Twenty-Four

Field. Day.

Some time after. **Young Woman** *stands looking around her. She mouths silently to herself.* **Gilbert** *appears.*

Gilbert   Day's over. You not walk back with the rest of the village? They say you speak to no one. Heard them talk about you at my mill. Works in the fields. Cares for the horses. Sits in her house at night. Not one word.

Young Woman   Why speak to any of them? Village believed me.

Gilbert   Broken-hearted wife.

Young Woman   Said all I needed to.

Gilbert   They never came for me.

Young Woman   You never ran.

Gilbert   Village'll find an empty mill tomorrow.

Young Woman   Where's the miller gone?

Gilbert   To the town won't call me 'miller'.

Young Woman   Have to walk far.

Gilbert   See more'f the world. Seen all this. Know all this. Nothing left for me. Every thing I have 's in here.

Young Woman   Things change every time I look at them. Each has a name.

Gilbert   Still see you. Every day I wake. Still hear his words.

Young Woman   So many names. I'll learn every one.

Gilbert   I want more. In the town there's books and pens and paper. Owned by people who've left villages. They speak all day about every thing in the world.

Young Woman   'S what you been told?

Gilbert   Have to believe some thing.

Young Woman   New things in my head. Every time I look. New names. Don't need somewhere else.

Gilbert   There's more the village's saying.

Young Woman   What?

Gilbert   Was you pulled the new horse out alone.

Young Woman   Horses trust me now.

Gilbert   You looked at it close?

Young Woman   'S a beautiful horse. Quick and strong.

Gilbert   Village's saying it's William. Say's Pony William running on the field.

Young Woman   Say more'n that. Say he's happier now than he ever was. Village's right. Pony is.

Gilbert   Here, horse-wife. Write what you know now. Write what you see.

He has given her the pen. He leaves.

Young Woman   Village needs a new miller.